ANIMAL PARTNERSHIPS

WRITTEN BY
Ben Hoare

ILLUSTRATED BY
Asia Orlando

Author Ben Hoare
Illustrator Asia Orlando
Consultant Dr Nick Crumpton
Editor Abi Maxwell
Senior Art Editor Charlotte Milner
Designers Bettina Myklebust Stovne, Brandie Tully-Scott, Victoria Palastanga
Senior Acquisitions Editor James Mitchem
Managing Art Editor Diane Peyton Jones
Production Editor Jacqueline Street-Elkayam
Production Controller Magdalena Bojko
Jacket and Sales Material Coordinator Elin Woosnam
Jacket Designer Charlotte Milner
Senior Picture Researcher Sakshi Saluja
Art Director Mabel Chan

First published in Great Britain in 2025 by
Dorling Kindersley Limited
20 Vauxhall Bridge Road,
London SW1V 2SA

The authorised representative in the EEA is
Dorling Kindersley Verlag GmbH. Arnulfstr. 124,
80636 Munich, Germany

Text copyright © Ben Hoare 2025
Illustrations © Asia Orlando 2025
Copyright in the layouts and design of
the Work shall be vested in the Publisher.
Dorling Kindersley Limited
DK, a Division of Penguin Random House LLC
10 9 8 7 6 5 4 3 2 1
001–349434–May/2025

All rights reserved.
No part of this publication may be reproduced, stored in or introduced into a retrieval system, or transmitted, in any form, or by any means (electronic, mechanical, photocopying, recording, or otherwise), without the prior written permission of the copyright owner.

A CIP catalogue record for this book
is available from the British Library.
ISBN: 978-0-2417-3989-1

Printed and bound in China

www.dk.com

This book was made with Forest Stewardship Council™ certified paper – one small step in DK's commitment to a sustainable future. Learn more at www.dk.com/uk/information/sustainability

CONTENTS

| INTRODUCTION | 4 |
| SYMBIOSIS | 6 |

FINDING FOOD — 8

TEAMING UP — 10
Orca, Harris's hawk, Dhole

FEASTING TOGETHER — 12
Common dolphin, Cape gannett, Bryde's whale, Copper shark, Humpback whale

ANT APPETITES — 14
Black garden ant & aphid, Red ant & Adonis blue butterfly, Purple hairstreak butterfly

COLONIAL HOMES — 16

BUSY BURROWS — 18
Gopher tortoise, Giant armadillo & ocelot

SAFE HOUSES — 20
Clownfish & anemone,
Glass sponge shrimp & Venus flower basket sponge,
Pygymy seahorse & sea fan

EVERYBODY TOGETHER — 22
Portuguese man-of-war, Apolemia uvaria

MOBILE PROTECTION — 24

HITCHING A RIDE — 26
Harlequin beetle & pseudoscorpion,
Burying beetle

ALL ABOARD — 28
Southern carmine bee-eater & kori bustard,
Whale barnacle & humpback whale
Dragonfly & Balkan terrapin

CLEANERS & DOCTORS 30

CLEANING STATIONS 32
Green turtle & surgeonfish,
Moon wrasse & manta ray

PERSONAL GROOMERS 34
Tiger shark & remora,
Black rhino & oxpecker, Hippo & barbel

RAISING YOUNG 36

YOUNGEST FIRST 38
African wild dog, Common marmoset

BABY BOOM 40
Ostrich, Banded mongoose, Long-tailed tit

SHARING THE LOAD 42
Termite colony, Damaraland mole rat

FIGHTING BACK 44

PROTECTIVE PARENTS 46
Musk ox, African elephant

CALLING IN THE MOB 48
Black-capped chickadee, blue jay & golden-crowned
kinglet, Capuchin monkey & squirrel monkey,
Cape ground squirrel

FEEDING PARASITES 50

SNATCH OF THE DAY 52
Arctic skua & Atlantic puffin, Spotted hyena

ZOMBIE HOSTS 54
Amber snail & trematode worm,
Cricket & horsehair worm, Cockroach wasp

BROOD PARASITES 56
Brown-headed cowbird & yellow warbler,
Horsfield's bronze cuckoo & superb fairywren,
Cuckoo paper wasp

GUARD ANIMALS 58

HONEY HUNTING 60
Greater honeyguide

FORAGING TOGETHER 62
Golden eagle, Irrawaddy dolphin,
Smooth-coated otter

ANIMALS & PLANTS 64

PLANT TOXINS 66
Monarch butterfly & milkweed plant,
Painted grasshopper

SEED DISPERSAL 68
Steller's jay, Red-rumped agouti, Orangutan

SETTLING IN 70
Mountain tree shrew, Gila woodpecker,
Red-eyed tree frog

BACTERIA BEST FRIENDS 72

THE CORAL & THE ALGAE 74
Coral polyp & zooxanthellae, Giant clam

CROP FARMING 76
Leafcutter ant, Dusky damselfish

INDEX 78
ACKNOWLEDGEMENTS 80

INTRODUCTION

Life can be tough for animals. They need to find food, water, and somewhere to live. They have to keep up with their friends and not get lost or separated. They have to breed somehow. And they must avoid their enemies. For wild animals, survival is far from easy!

Faced with these challenges, animals have come up with some clever tricks to survive. One of their smartest ideas is to form a partnership with other animals and work together as a team. If you think about it, we humans do much the same thing when we're in a sticky situation. We look for our best friends and seek out allies who can help us.

The intriguing partnerships that animals develop are what this book is all about. As you will discover, there are lots of these partnerships in nature. They involve creatures everywhere on Earth, from the deepest ocean to the highest mountain, and from the icy poles to tropical forests. Sometimes, animals form associations with plants and microscopic algae, too.

Animal partnerships can be complicated at times, just like human friendships. But they are always special, and I can't wait to tell you about them. Are you ready? Then let's go!

– BEN HOARE

COMMENSALISM

Here, one species wins, and the other neither wins nor loses. For example, a jackdaw will often land on a sheep to tug out tufts of wool. The bird needs the wool for its nest. The sheep, meanwhile, does not come to any harm. In fact, it may hardly feel a thing.

MUTUALISM

Both parties benefit here. When a hawk moth visits flowers to sip their nectar, it gets an energy boost, but the flowers win, too. The hawk moth helps to spread their pollen.

SYMBIOSIS

We have a name for close relationships that develop between different species: symbiosis (you say it "sim-bye-oh-sis"). There are three main types of symbiosis. A relationship that helps both species is called mutualism. When just one species benefits, we call it commensalism. And if one benefits and the other suffers, it is known as parasitism. In addition, members of the same species may form incredible partnerships. These friendships are not symbiosis, but are still fascinating.

COLONIAL

Some species breed in groups, or colonies, often because they are safer in large numbers. Great dusky swifts, for example, nest together on the rocky cliffs behind waterfalls in South America. This type of colonial behaviour is common in birds, mammals, and amphibians, and is also found in many marine animals.

UNDECIDED

It's hard to know what category some newly discovered pairings belong in. The tadpoles of the golden poison frog develop in the tiny pools of water that form in the centre of bromeliad plants. Scientists used to think that this made no difference to the plant, and was a case of commensalism. Now, some wonder if the frog poo may benefit the plant, which would make it mutualism.

PARASITISM

Here, one species benefits at the expense of another. The harmful species is known as a parasite. The blue rockfish is a parasite, because it steals prey from jellyfish, which lose their meal. This example is called kleptoparasitism. Parasitism can also involve tricking another species, or feeding on their flesh or blood.

EUSOCIAL

Eusocial relationships are a very special kind of colonial living, where a single female controls a colony made up of other members of her species. Ants, termites, and some bees and wasps are eusocial. Their nests are ruled by a powerful queen, the only female in the colony that breeds.

SOOTY TERN

MACKEREL

YELLOWFIN TUNA

FISH SUPPER

Sooty terns are fish-eating seabirds and they have a problem: oceans are ENORMOUS. So, how do they find their fish supper? One way is to follow yellowfin tuna on the hunt. These speedy fish chase smaller fish such as mackerel. As the mackerel try to escape, they panic and leap out of the water. Big mistake... the terns are flying right above, waiting to catch them!

FINDING FOOD

When we're feeling peckish, we head to the kitchen or go shopping. Animals aren't so lucky – locating their next meal is a challenge. But if they hang out with a different species, then sourcing a snack sometimes becomes a whole lot easier...

WILD BOAR

PLAYING TAG

European robins love nothing better than a juicy beetle or earthworm. To catch their favourite food, they have a sneaky trick. If they spot wild boar in a forest, they tag along. When the boar rummage through piles of leaves to find their own food, this disturbs a host of small creatures and gives the robins a meal, too.

EUROPEAN ROBIN

8

FINDING FOOD

ARCTIC FOX

POLAR BEAR

FOLLOW MY LEADER
You will often see an Arctic fox following in the footsteps of a polar bear, but what is it up to? After all, the bear could kill the fox with one swipe of a mighty paw! Luckily, polar bears prefer to eat seals and whales, and don't mind being followed. So, when the bear makes a kill, it's safe for the fox to tuck into the leftovers.

BIG BROWN BAT

A BITE TO EAT
On summer nights, white-tailed deer are bothered by swarms of biting flies. However, the deer have unlikely friends – big brown bats. After dark, the bats swoop around the deer and catch as many flies as they can. The bats enjoy their dinner, and with fewer flies about, the deer are bitten less. Both the bats and the deer benefit from this relationship.

Biting flies have scissor-like mouthparts, brilliant for stabbing mammals like deer, so they can sip on their blood!

BITING DEER FLIES

WHITE-TAILED DEER

9

TEAMING UP

There is a popular saying: many hands make light work. What this means is that some things in life are much simpler if you tackle them as a team. Likewise, many predators use teamwork to catch their prey.

Orcas peer above water to "spyhop" their prey – a seal on some ice.

WOLVES OF THE SEA
Orcas are highly social animals. They spend their whole lives in groups, known as pods, led by a grandmother orca, the matriarch. Each pod specializes in hunting a different type of prey. For example, a few pods of orcas in Antarctica have a unique method of catching seals. For it to succeed, their timing has to be perfect.

WEDDELL SEAL

WAVE WASHING
First, the orcas search for a seal resting on an ice floe (a chunk of floating sea ice). They plan their attack, then charge. The force of their approach sends a huge wave crashing over the seal and the ice. If necessary, they regroup and repeat the move, until at last the seal is washed into the sea. Now it stands no chance against the orcas.

Forming a line, the orcas rush towards their target...

...and the wave they create flings the seal into the water.

TEAMING UP

SCARE TACTICS

Most birds of prey hunt alone. Harris's hawks are different, though. Groups of up to six of these birds will join a hunt. Often, they take turns to fly ahead to scare a jackrabbit from its hiding place. Meanwhile, the other hawks wait nearby. When the frightened animal runs into the open, they swoop to seize it. After a successful hunt, the hawks share the food.

HARRIS'S HAWK

DHOLE

The forests of southern Asia are home to a wild dog called the dhole (you say it "dole"). They live in packs of up to 12 members. When hunting deer in the thick forests, the pack members frequently lose sight of one another. So, they whistle to stay in touch and coordinate their group attack.

BRAINY BIRDS

Teamwork requires intelligence and quick thinking. And because Harris's hawks are team players that learn fast, we can train them. Some people keep these trained hawks to catch rabbits and rats. The hawks are also used at airports to scare away flocks of geese and other birds, which could cause an accident if they hit an aircraft.

The rest of the group swoop down and seize their prey.

One hawk flies ahead to flush a jackrabbit out into the open.

11

FEASTING TOGETHER

Fishing takes patience and skill, as anyone who has tried it will tell you. Fish-eating animals know this, too. Instead of fishing alone, which is hard work, they round up the fish together, like farmers herding sheep.

SILVERY SHOALS

Every June and July, vast numbers of sardines swim north along the coast of southern Africa. The great journey made by these little fish has a nickname – the Sardine Run – and it is a stunning spectacle. The huge shoals can be up to 5 km (3 miles) wide and 20 km (12.5 miles) long! But the billions of fish do not go unnoticed...

COMMON DOLPHINS

MOVING AS ONE

Thousands of common dolphins follow the sardines. They split into groups, dive under the fish, then zoom upwards at them. This forces the sardines to bunch up at the surface. Each swirling mass of fish is called a bait ball. By forming a ball, the sardines make it difficult for the dolphins to target them. Many will still be caught, but enough survive to continue their journey.

BRYDE'S WHALE

CAPE GANNETS

FEASTING TOGETHER

JOINING THE FEAST
Dolphins are not the only ocean predators with an eye on the sardines. Cape fur seals, as well as copper sharks and even a few Bryde's whales (you say their name "broo-dus" whales) also join the attack. At the same time, Cape gannets launch strikes from the sky. Flocks of these sharp-beaked seabirds dive down into the shoals of fish like missiles.

SARDINES

COPPER SHARK

HUMPBACK WHALE
Some humpback whales that visit the coast of North America have a special fishing technique. Several whales swim in a circle, blowing bubbles with the blowholes on their heads. Soon, the water is full of noisy bubbles, which confuses any fish. The whales keep blowing bubbles until the fish are surrounded. Finally, they lunge at the fish to gulp them down.

APHID

BLACK GARDEN ANT

UNLIKELY PARTNERS
Black garden ants spend a lot of time with tiny insects called aphids, which have a surprising secret. As the aphids graze on plants, they produce a waste product rich in sugar. Eating another animal's waste might sound disgusting, but the ants adore what comes out of the rear ends of the aphids! To ensure a regular supply, they guard the little aphids from predators.

Aphids have many predators, including ladybirds and wasps.

ANT FARMERS
The sweet stuff aphids produce is called honeydew. And the ants love it so much, they don't just protect the aphids, they also keep them clean. Even more amazing, the ants carry the aphids to fresh new plants to make sure they always have plenty to eat. If you think about it, the ants are a bit like dairy farmers. Rather than milking cows, they "milk" aphids instead!

ANT APPETITES

Some people have a sweet tooth, and it's the same with ants. To get their sweet treats, these ants have developed an extraordinary partnership with other insects. They know that if they help the insects, they will receive a sugary reward that makes it all worth it.

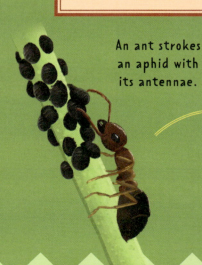

An ant strokes an aphid with its antennae.

In response, the aphid releases honeydew.

ANT APPETITES

RED ANT   ADONIS BLUE CATERPILLAR

TAP AND SIP

Red ants live in grasslands, where they look for a particular kind of caterpillar. The one they are after is the green-and-yellow caterpillar of the Adonis blue butterfly. At one end of this caterpillar's body is something called a honey gland. When the ants tap it, a sugary substance trickles out, similar to aphid honeydew. As with the honeydew, the ants can't resist it!

LOVING CARE

It's dangerous being a juicy caterpillar, as many other creatures want to eat you. So, to thank it for giving them "honey", the ants guard it around the clock. When the caterpillar is ready to pupate and transform into a butterfly, they take it into their nest. They keep the pupa safe, like loving parents tucking up a child.

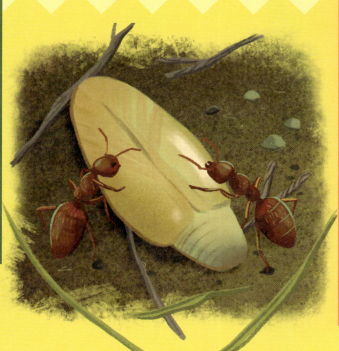

Red ants care for a caterpillar pupa in their nest.

PURPLE HAIRSTREAK

It's not just ants that have a sweet tooth – butterflies do, too. Unlike most other butterflies, the purple hairstreak does not usually visit flowers to sip nectar. It has a stranger diet: the honeydew made by aphids. To find the makers of this golden liquid, it flies to the top of oak trees where the aphids are feeding.

COLONIAL HOMES

For some animals, living together makes sense... but not because they get lonely on their own! It's just that in groups, they're better at finding food, making homes, or fighting off enemies. They may form large groups of the same species, called colonies. Or they may share their living space with different species entirely.

COMMON WASP NEST

PAPER PALACES

Many wasps live in colonies with thousands of workers, all female. Every colony is controlled by a single female, the queen. The wasps construct a beautiful hanging nest for the colony's eggs and young. It is made from tiny strips of wood that they mix with spit to make a pulp. When dry, this creates a papery structure – the wasp version of papier-mâché.

STICKING TOGETHER

In Africa, colonies of sparrow-sized birds called sociable weavers build massive stick nests on trees and even on telegraph poles. There may be 100 families sharing a nest, with each family in their own nesting chamber. A pair of pygmy falcons may move in to share the nest, too! The falcons help to protect the nest, and get a cosy home in return.

SOCIABLE WEAVER BIRD NEST

16

COLONIAL HOMES

TERMITE TOWERS

Termites are ant-like insects that love being in a crowd. In fact, there can be a million termites in one of their colonies! But you rarely ever see the termites, because they mostly feed underground and live in a humongous mound. They build it from earth, dry grass, and their own spit. The hot Sun bakes the mound until it's as hard as concrete.

Termites are the main food of giant anteaters, which can eat more than 30,000 of them a day!

TERMITE NESTS

GROUND SQUIRREL BURROW

UNDER THE SURFACE

In the natural grasslands of North America, known as prairies, trees are few and far between. There are barely any places to hide. So, where do you set up home if you're a squirrel? Underground! Ground squirrels dig big burrows in the prairies, with numerous passages, chambers, and entrances. Each is shared by 20 or more squirrels.

GOPHER TORTOISE

HOME SWEET HOME

The gopher tortoise is found in the southeast USA, but much of the time it lives below ground. Its powerful front feet are like shovels – just the job for digging with. When it gets to work, this industrious tortoise quickly makes a burrow that eventually stretches several metres in every direction. The largest tortoise burrows are as long as a double-decker bus!

BUSY BURROWS

Animals that own big homes often end up sharing their living quarters. The gopher tortoise is one such animal. Its spacious burrow has more than enough room for other species to move in. These lodgers benefit from free accommodation, yet are no problem for the tortoise.

More than 350 species of animal make use of gopher tortoise burrows.

BUSY BURROWS

BURROWING OWL

WELCOME GUESTS

All sorts of animals will make use of a tortoise burrow. Depending on the time of year, they might include owls, mice, frogs, small lizards, a weasel-like mammal known as the spotted skunk, and insects such as crickets. The lodger you would least expect to be here is the eastern diamondback rattlesnake. Though venomous, it hunts elsewhere and gets along fine with the other residents.

FLORIDA MOUSE

HIDDEN BENEFITS

The animals living in a tortoise burrow are protected from summer heat and winter cold, as well as from predators and bush fires. Some of them stay only a short while, but others actually raise a family in the burrow. Several beetles and flies live only in these burrows – you'll find them nowhere else on Earth.

CAVE CRICKET

EASTERN DIAMONDBACK RATTLESNAKE

GOPHER FROG

GOPHER TORTOISE ROVE BEETLE

MOLE SKINK

SPOTTED SKUNK

GIANT ARMADILLO & OCELOT

South America's giant armadillos cannot stop digging! They excavate new burrows every couple of days, and the old ones are a lifesaver for other animals. Ocelots, much like miniature leopards, use the armadillo dens to escape the scorching Sun.

TIGER BEETLE

19

SAFE HOUSES

Oceans teem with hungry mouths. If you happen to be on the small side, it's a perilous place to be. No wonder some tiddly fish and shrimps have decided they need high-security houses. Their homes are... other animals!

TOXIC TENTACLES

Clownfish live with anemones, which resemble clumps of weird spaghetti. Like jellyfish, the anemones have tentacles armed with stingers to paralyse prey. But the clownfish don't get stung, because their skin is covered in mucus, which forms a slimy coat of armour. So, they can swim happily among the lethal tentacles, where predators can't reach them.

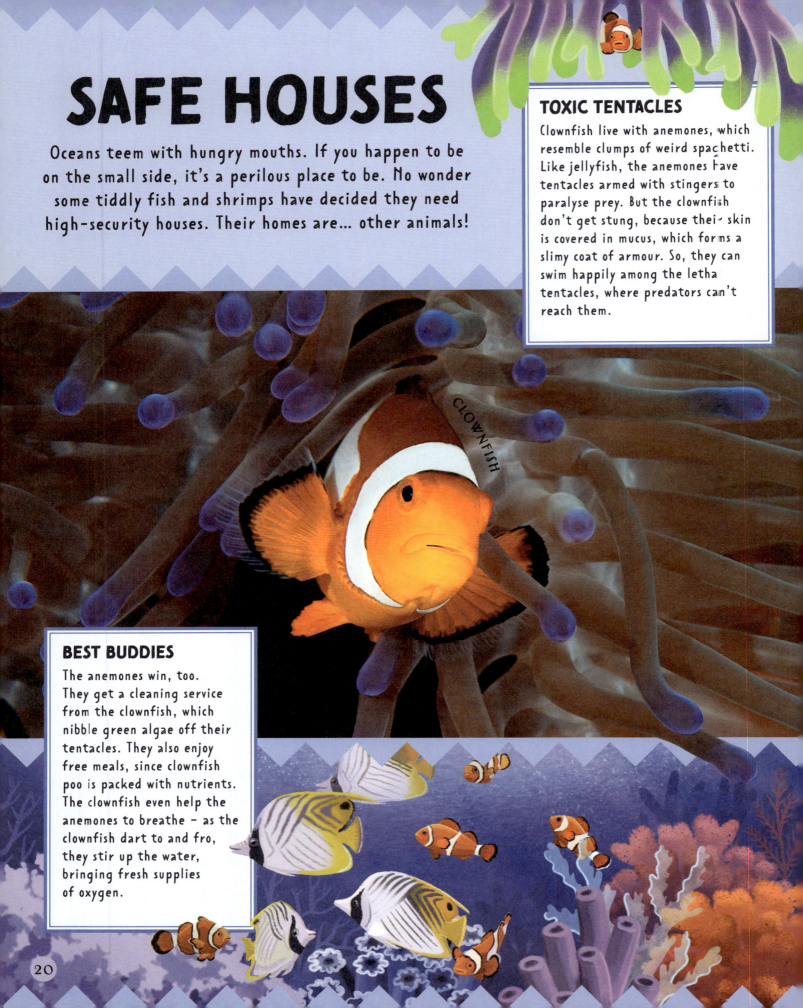

CLOWNFISH

BEST BUDDIES

The anemones win, too. They get a cleaning service from the clownfish, which nibble green algae off their tentacles. They also enjoy free meals, since clownfish poo is packed with nutrients. The clownfish even help the anemones to breathe – as the clownfish dart to and fro, they stir up the water, bringing fresh supplies of oxygen.

GLASS HOUSES

The deep ocean is full of curious creatures, including Venus's flower baskets. These are a type of glass sponge, with see-through skeletons, like cages made of glass. To feed, they draw in water through the holes in their skeletons to extract tiny scraps of food. But this also sucks in young glass sponge shrimps. Once inside, they make themselves at home.

SAFE HOUSES

GLASS SPONGE SHRIMP

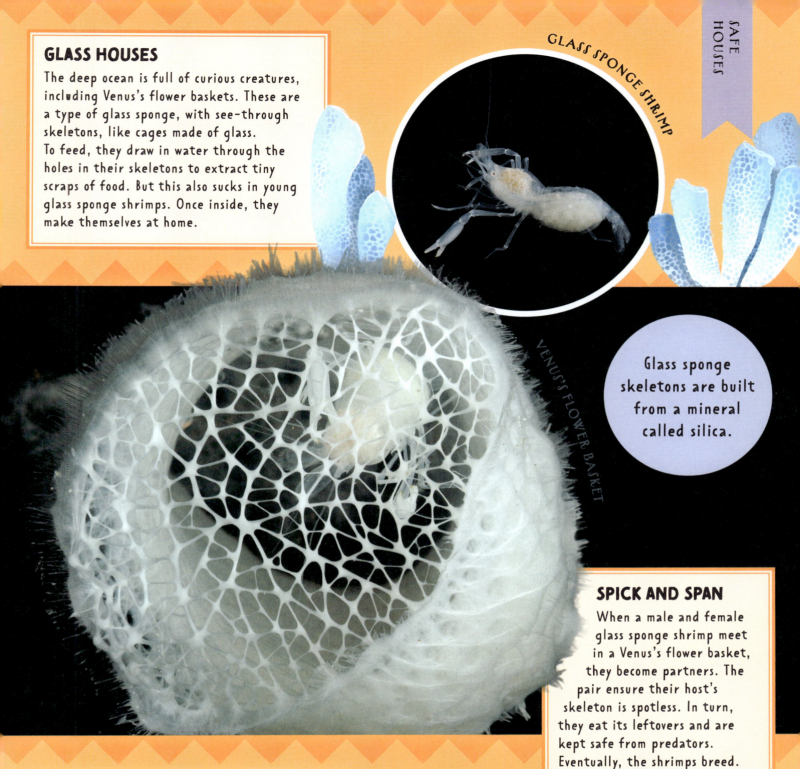

VENUS'S FLOWER BASKET

Glass sponge skeletons are built from a mineral called silica.

SPICK AND SPAN

When a male and female glass sponge shrimp meet in a Venus's flower basket, they become partners. The pair ensure their host's skeleton is spotless. In turn, they eat its leftovers and are kept safe from predators. Eventually, the shrimps breed. Their tiny young swim out through the holes in the skeleton, to find Venus's flower baskets of their own. But, by now, the parent shrimps have grown too big to escape. They remain inside for the rest of their lives!

PYGMY SEAHORSE

These minuscule animals never stray far from sea fans, which seem to be plants but in fact are animals related to corals. They copy the appearance of their sea fan homes so well, their enemies can't see them. The sea fans don't gain anything, but aren't harmed either.

EVERYBODY TOGETHER

Swimming in the ocean, there are living things that are not what they at first seem. These wonders of nature APPEAR to be a single animal, but really are lots of separate animals that share the same body.

ONE BIG TEAM

The organisms that live like this include siphonophores (you say their name "sai-fon-oh-fors"). They have a soft body divided into many parts. Each part is an individual animal, called a zooid. The zooids do a range of different jobs for the organism. They might catch prey, for example. They also help it to move, digest things, reproduce, or defend itself.

OCEAN DRIFTER

Some siphonophores look similar to jellyfish. Among them is the Portuguese man-of-war. It drifts at the surface of the ocean, thanks to its floating "bag" full of gases. Below this, there are many long stinging tentacles, which trail through the water. Any fish or shrimps that touch them are stung, paralysed with venom, and pulled into the main body to be eaten.

The Portuguese man-of-war has no brain, yet the animals in its body work brilliantly as a team.

FLOATING ZOOIDS

These create a kind of bag or balloon, which keeps the colony afloat and helps it to sail across the sea.

BREEDING ZOOIDS

When the colony is ready to breed, these zooids release eggs or sperm into the water to be fertlized.

FEEDING ZOOIDS

The role of these zooids is to digest food. Each one is like a stomach, with its own mouth.

HUNTING ZOOIDS

These form the twirling tentacles, which fire threads out to sting and paralyse prey.

PORTUGUESE MAN-OF-WAR

EVERYBODY TOGETHER

FISHY COMPANION

The tentacles of a Portuguese man-of-war are a lovely blue colour, but don't be fooled. The venom in their stings could kill a human! Fortunately, such deaths are rare. Incredibly, however, there are fish that call them home. Young bluebottle fish hide among the tentacles, receiving protection from them while eating bits of food that float past.

BLUEBOTTLE FISH

APOLEMIA UVARIA

Like the Portuguese man-of-war, this life form is a siphonophore. It's like a gloopy mass of pink, blue, or white string. When fully extended, its body can be the length of a tennis court. But the longest on record was thought to be around 120 m (394 ft) long!

23

FANCY DRESS

Sea urchins bristle with vicious spines that are loaded with venom. This means these animals are a nasty mouthful for fish – and the ideal accessory for a defenceless decorator crab. Using its rear two pairs of legs, the crab heaves an urchin onto its shell, leaving its front two pairs for walking. It's protected from predators such as octopuses, and the sea urchin gets to travel the seabed to new feeding areas, so it's a win-win!

DECORATOR CRAB

MOBILE PROTECTION

Moving around the ocean can be hazardous for many sea creatures. Out in the open water, away from their usual hiding places, predators may strike. If they call in backup to increase their security, they have no need to worry.

SUITS OF ARMOUR

Long ago, the ancestors of hermit crabs gradually changed shape. They ended up losing their own shells, but would squeeze into the empty shells of sea snails and wear those for protection instead. For millions of years, this snail armour kept them safe. Today, however, hermit crabs also climb into bottle caps and other pieces of plastic rubbish left on beaches. Sadly, these artificial shelters are much less suitable.

HERMIT CRAB

MOBILE PROTECTION

PAPER NAUTILUS OCTOPUS

STING IN THE TALE

The paper nautilus is a very unusual octopus. Unlike most octopuses, it drifts near the surface of the sea. Here, it is exposed to many dangers, but it latches onto a jellyfish, whose stinging tentacles protect it. We once thought this passenger did the jellyfish no harm... Not any more. Now we know it may bite holes in the jellyfish to suck out the contents of its last meal. So, it's also a parasite!

The sneaky paper nautilus can steer its jellyfish in different directions.

GOLIATH GROUPER

DIVE BUDDY

When fully grown, a goliath grouper weighs nearly as much as a grand piano. Legends claim it swallows the odd human! These stories are probably not true. This mean-looking fish does, however, stuff its colossal jaws with lobsters, fish, baby turtles, and much more. Little fish have realized it's the perfect bodyguard – and they have nothing to fear, as they're too small for the grouper to consider eating.

25

HARLEQUIN BEETLE

Pseudoscorpions strap themselves to their beetle with "seatbelts" made from sticky silk.

HITCHING A RIDE

For teeny animals smaller than a grain of rice, every log must seem like a mountain. Getting around is a pain, especially if the animals can't fly. But there's a solution at hand – they can piggyback on larger animals. This behaviour is called phoresy.

HOLD TIGHT

To see phoresy in action, let's visit a tropical forest in South America. On a fig tree, there are tiny creatures scurrying around. These are pseudoscorpions (relatives of spiders, not real scorpions). Here's the clever bit. To reach new trees, they wait until a beetle, such as this harlequin beetle, appears... and climb on board! They crawl under its wings, using their sharp claws to hold on.

PSEUDOSCORPION

HITCHING A RIDE

PSEUDOSCORPION

BURYING BEETLE

This handsome beetle buries dead animals for its young to eat. As it flies between these smelly meals, it transports dozens of red mites on its back, without even knowing it. Like the beetle, the little mites need dead animals for their young to eat.

SAFE LANDING

When the beetle touches down, its rowdy passengers disembark. The female pseudoscorpions jump off onto the fig tree, where their eggs will produce a new generation of pseudoscorpions. But before the beetle flies off, it unwittingly accepts a new load of pseudoscorpions. And the pushing and shoving starts all over again...

IN-FLIGHT ANTICS

The harlequin beetle flies to a different part of the forest, carrying several pseudoscorpions with it. Do they relax during the flight? No way! They are likely to get into fights. The biggest male tries to shove other males off the beetle. He is trying to make sure he's the only male left, so that he can mate with the female pseudoscorpions also on the flight.

27

ALL ABOARD

What's the most important thing to take on a journey? Snacks, of course! Meet the animals that travel in style, by catching a ride on a bigger beast to enjoy a non-stop supply of nibbles.

BEE-WARE!

The southern carmine bee-eater lives in the African savannah and feeds on – you guessed it – bees. Its usual hunting tactic is to sit on a perch, wait patiently for a bee or wasp to fly past, then chase after the insect. But what if its perch could MOVE? Then it could search a much wider area. Enter the kori bustard, which looks like a cross between a heron and a turkey.

EARLY WARNING

As the great bird stomps about to search for its own prey, its huge feet disturb bees and wasps that the bee-eater can snatch while riding on its back. What's in it for the bustard? One theory is that when the bee-eater spots an eagle or some other predator, its calls may alert the bustard to the danger.

BEE-EATER

KORI BUSTARD

The bustard disturbs insects that the bee-eater grabs.

DRAGONFLY

When a Balkan terrapin surfaces in a pond, a passing dragonfly seizes its chance. It whizzes over and lands on the terrapin's head! Cheeky maybe, but the terrapin makes a convenient lookout, from which the dragonfly can scan the water for its mosquito prey.

WHALE OF A TIME

Humpback whales cruising the ocean are rarely alone. Many have hitchhikers – whale barnacles. These are like barnacles found on rocks, but they live only on whales. As the whales swim along, the whale barnacles stick out feathery feet to capture particles of food. The whales visit parts of the ocean rich in food, so their lucky passengers never go hungry.

ALL ABOARD

HUMPBACK WHALE

A HEAVY LOAD

Whale barnacles begin their lives as microscopic young, or larvae. The larvae swim in the ocean, until they bump into a whale. Most creep towards the whale's mouth or flippers, where they dig into the skin and grow a shell. Firmly attached, they stick with the whale for life. The poor whale gets nothing in return – and its heavy load of barnacles may actually slow it down!

Whale barnacle larvae detect the smell of a whale.

They swim over and climb on.

Their feathery feet poke out to feed from its back.

BARNACLES FEEDING

Each species of whale has a different species of whale barnacle living on it.

WORKER HONEYBEES

CLEANING CREW

In a honeybee hive, there's much work to do. The thousands of worker bees are highly organized and divide the tasks between them. Some are specialist cleaners, whose role is to remove dirt from the nest and polish the cells in which eggs and young bees are developing. They do this for the first two weeks of their life, then are promoted to doing other jobs for the hive, like collecting pollen and nectar.

CAIMAN AND BUTTERFLY

CROCODILE TEARS

Caimans are toothy reptiles that – like crocodiles, to which they are related – frequently appear to be crying. But they're not sad. Their "tears" give their eyes a wash and get rid of unwanted salt in their body. Spotting an opportunity, butterflies sip the droplets to top up their own levels of salt and other minerals, which they can't obtain from their nectar diet. It doesn't seem to bother the caimans one bit.

In addition to butterflies, bees also sip tears and sweat from other animals – and even from humans!

CLEANERS & DOCTORS

Animals can take their personal hygiene VERY seriously. They may spend ages tidying their homes, keeping themselves clean, and looking after their health. We even know of an insect that carries out life-saving surgery on its friends!

EMERGENCY SURGERY

We used to think that only humans were able to perform surgery. But, in 2024, scientists discovered that Florida carpenter ants operate on each other! When an ant injured a leg, other ants in its nest cleaned the wound or chewed the entire leg off. Sounds drastic, but amputating the leg stopped the wound getting infected. And, amazingly, the now five-legged ant usually survived.

EUROPEAN BADGER

FLORIDA CARPENTER ANTS

MAKING THEIR BEDS

European badgers live in large groups, like extended families, each of which shares a burrow called a sett. You might expect living underground to be a messy business, yet the badgers are extremely house-proud and regularly change their family's bedding. They roll dry grass into a ball and drag it underground to sleep on, and dump the dirty old bedding outside the sett.

CLEANING STATIONS

Once in a while, sea turtles and fish like to treat themselves to a proper wash and brush up. So, they book themselves a session at a cleaning station – the ocean's equivalent of a health spa. Afterwards, they feel much better for it.

An old green turtle recognizes this part of the reef from previous visits.

SPA DAY

Green turtles are named for the greenish colour of their flesh. However, their shells also turn green with algae. The algae is a nuisance – it slows them down. To get rid of it, the turtles visit a "spa" they know on the coral reef, where yellow tangs are waiting. These fish use their pointed mouths to graze on the algae and scrape the turtle shells clean.

The turtle swims into position to be cleaned.

MOON WRASSE & MANTA RAY

Manta rays are some of the biggest fish in the sea. When they visit cleaning stations, they're met by moon wrasse, which swarm eagerly over them from head to tail fin. The little wrasse are even bold enough to clean inside the gill slits and mouths of the grateful rays, as well as any wounds.

32

CLEANING STATIONS

SURGEONFISH WITH A WRASSE

TAKING TURNS

Cleaning stations on the reef are busy places, with customers queuing up for their turn. An array of fish beauticians work here – in addition to yellow tangs, there may be damselfish, angelfish, and wrasse. The smaller fish also help to clean the larger cleaners. They move all over the bodies of their clients to scoff any algae, dead skin, loose scales, and parasites they come across.

GREEN TURTLE

HEALTHY REEFS

Every section of a coral reef has a cleaning station, and it may have been in use for a long time. Sometimes you can actually see where the coral or rock has been worn smooth by all the visiting turtles and fish over the years! Many of the cleaner fish, such as yellow tangs, graze algae off the coral, too. This means the cleaning station benefits the reef as a whole.

Turtles and fish swim in a special way to announce they want to be cleaned.

33

PERSONAL GROOMERS

Film stars take make-up assistants with them on set, and they're not the only ones. Many animals also love to be pampered on the go. But there's a crucial difference – for their personal groomers, this is snack time.

FISHY FRIENDS

A large shark often has smaller fish, called remoras, swarming around it, like little boats circling a big cruise liner. You might think the remoras are taking a risk by making friends with a deadly predator. However, it's them, not the shark, that are thinking of dinner! They grab scraps of food left over from the shark's meals, and remove tasty parasites from its skin and gills.

TIGER SHARK

REMORA

DON'T LET GO

Both the shark and the remoras are winners in this relationship. The shark receives a body scrub, while the remoras benefit from a free meal and a free rice. Remoras are weak swimmers, so getting a lift is a huge help. They cling on using a suction cup behind their head. This sucker was once a fin, but has adapted to become something even more useful.

BIG ATTRACTION

Black rhinos can't help attracting crowds of starling-sized birds. Their admirers are red-billed oxpeckers, which are irresistibly drawn to rhinos and other grazing animals in the African savannah. The big draw? Food – in the form of ticks, fleas, crusty old skin, dry blood, or even earwax. The oxpeckers scamper wherever they like on their four-legged transport, feeding to their heart's content.

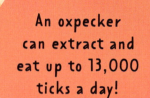

PERSONAL GROOMERS

BLACK RHINO

An oxpecker can extract and eat up to 13,000 ticks a day!

RED-BILLED OXPECKER

TURNING NASTY

As a bonus, the oxpeckers are watchful birds that call out if they see lions or hyenas – useful for rhino mums who need to protect their vulnerable babies. But there's a catch. Sometimes, the oxpeckers use their scissor-shaped beaks to peck at open wounds on their rhino hosts. They have turned into bloodsucking parasites, and are not so friendly now!

HIPPO & BARBEL

Hippos have smooth folds of skin that attract all manner of parasites. Luckily, the moment they dive into a pool, they are surrounded by barbel fish. The barbels have wide mouths with teeth like cheese graters, with which they scrape off every last parasite. They also pick off (and eat) dung from the hippos' mucky backsides!

35

RAISING YOUNG

Caring for babies is hugely demanding, so some animals drop their young off at nurseries, or "crèches". It frees the parents up to do other important stuff, such as hunt for food, while helpers take over the parenting until their return.

ROYAL TERN CHICK

PENGUIN PARADE

At first, an emperor penguin chick snuggles under its mum or dad to stay warm. By seven weeks old, it joins a crèche with all the other chicks, which allows both its parents to go fishing. While the adult penguins are away, the chicks form a giant huddle against the cold, guarded by a handful of grown-ups. When the parents reappear, they know which chick to feed because they recognize its call.

BONDING ON THE BEACH

Royal terns breed on sandy beaches in large groups, or colonies, where their screechy cries fill the air. The chicks leave their nests at just a day or two old and cram together in a crèche, overseen by several adult terns. It's a squeeze! But the mass of fluffy bodies confuses predators such as foxes or gulls, which struggle to single out a target.

EMPEROR PENGUIN CHICKS

RAISING YOUNG

BLACK-AND-WHITE RUFFED LEMUR BABIES

TREETOP NURSERY

A wide variety of mammal mums leave their young in a "nursery" for short periods. Bats do it, and so do giraffes, various monkeys, and several wild species in the dog family. On the island of Madagascar, black-and-white ruffed lemurs do it, too. Two or three lemur mums park their babies up in a leafy nest in the treetops, with another adult member of their group left in charge.

Some flamingo crèches contain tens of thousands of chicks.

GREATER FLAMINGO CHICK

SAFETY IN NUMBERS

Flamingos nest on shallow lakes in huge flocks. While the pink parents head off to feed, the fluffy grey chicks assemble together in the largest crèches on Earth! The chicks swim and paddle around in the mud, but there are some adults around to keep order. It is safer being in a crowd. If an eagle attacks, it can only take one chick at a time, so most will escape.

YOUNGEST FIRST

On the plains of Africa, you will find awesome hunters that live in groups of up to 40. These are not lions, but African wild dogs. Unlike the big cats, in a wild dog pack everyone takes great care of the young.

WAIT YOUR TURN!

When lions bring down prey, it's the adult males that feed first. Lionesses eat next, and the cubs are last in the pecking order. If they're unlucky, they are just left with scraps. But with African wild dogs, it's the other way round! The youngest members of the pack tuck into the meat first. Not until they have filled their faces do the older dogs then take their turn.

African wild dogs chase a wildebeest to tire it out.

Success! They whistle the others over to share the meal.

Later, some of the hunters bring up meat for the pups.

BABYSITTERS

African wild dogs catch their prey, such as antelopes and buffalo, after a fast and furious chase. It may go on for as long as 20 minutes. The pups can't keep up, so they remain behind. One or more adults of the pack stay with them as babysitters. After a kill, dogs on the hunt return to the den, where they bring up, or regurgitate, meat for the pups and babysitters.

AFRICAN WILD DOG AND PUP

YOUNGEST FIRST

TOP TWO
A pack's top-ranking pair of dogs, the alpha male and female, are generally the only ones that breed. They're assisted by the other adults. What's in it for them? If they are related to the pups, they benefit because they are helping their relatives, which have some of the same genes. If they are not related, they still win, because they are helping the pack grow, and larger packs have more hunting success.

If an African wild dog is injured, the rest of the pack feed it until it recovers.

COMMON MARMOSET
These monkeys usually have twins, and the mum and dad get help from other adults to rear their babies. Some helpers are more use than others! The really helpful ones play with and clean the babies, and if they are female, may even suckle the infants on their own milk.

BABY BOOM

Some animals grow up surrounded by a gaggle of siblings and mates. The youngsters come into the world within hours or days of each other, which makes it easier for the adults to keep them out of harm's way.

MUM
DAD
CHICKS

EGGSTRAORDINARY NEST

An ostrich nest may have 20 or more enormous eggs in it. They belong to different females, only one of which stays to guard the nest, helped by a male. If the ostriches had several nests, egg thieves such as baboons (a kind of monkey) would probably find at least one of them. But because there is just a single nest, the thieves are more likely to miss it.

Ostriches lay the world's largest eggs. Each weighs the same as 24 chicken eggs!

SUPERMUM AND SUPERDAD

After six weeks, the eggs in the nest begin hatching, and the male and female ostrich soon lead the chicks away. Sometimes the pair meet other ostriches with huge broods of their own. The different broods may merge, so one pair ends up with a megabrood. This incredible mum and dad might be responsible for as many as 300 chicks!

OSTRICH

BABY BOOM

THE MONGOOSE MOB

Banded mongooses do EVERYTHING together. They scurry about in a noisy rabble, always chirping and chattering, like excited classmates on a school trip. The females in each group give birth around the same time, so there can suddenly be a dozen or so babies in the mongoose den. Several males babysit the boisterous cubs while the rest of the gang go hunting.

MALE BABYSITTERS

LITTERS OF BABIES

BANDED MONGOOSE

MOVING HOME

Every few days, the mongooses move their cubs to a new den in another part of their territory. Mongooses have many predators, from birds of prey to hyenas, which might smell them if they stayed put. Forever moving home is the safest thing to do. The cubs have loose fur on their backs, so being picked up in the mouth of an adult mongoose is not as painful as it looks!

LONG-TAILED TIT

In spring, long-tailed tits have up to 12 chicks to feed. It's a lot for the parents to cope with! But other long-tailed tits often come to their aid. These helpers are birds that were not able to raise their own family, and they bring extra meals of insects and spiders for the chicks. Scientists have discovered that the helpers are usually male. They may be brothers of either parent.

HELPER MALE

BREEDING FEMALE

BREEDING MALE

SHARING THE LOAD

Imagine living with thousands of brothers and sisters! That's what it is like in a termite colony. All the young belong to a powerful queen, so every termite is related. The termites join forces to care for newly hatched eggs in order to grow the colony.

TASKMASTERS

We call the termites' way of life "eusocial". For it to be a success, the thousands of termites have to cooperate – and here's their secret... Their mound is like a busy factory inside, because it's full of workers that all have different jobs! Every termite is adapted to carry out a specific task, so is an expert at what it does underground to establish their colony.

TERMITE SOLDIER

JOB DESCRIPTIONS

Many of the worker termites are foragers that gather food. Others are nurses that tend to the queen and the larvae, or young. Then there are construction workers that build and repair the mound, and caretakers that keep it neat and tidy. A special group of termites act as soldiers. They are several times larger than the workers, with massive jaws to fight and defend the colony.

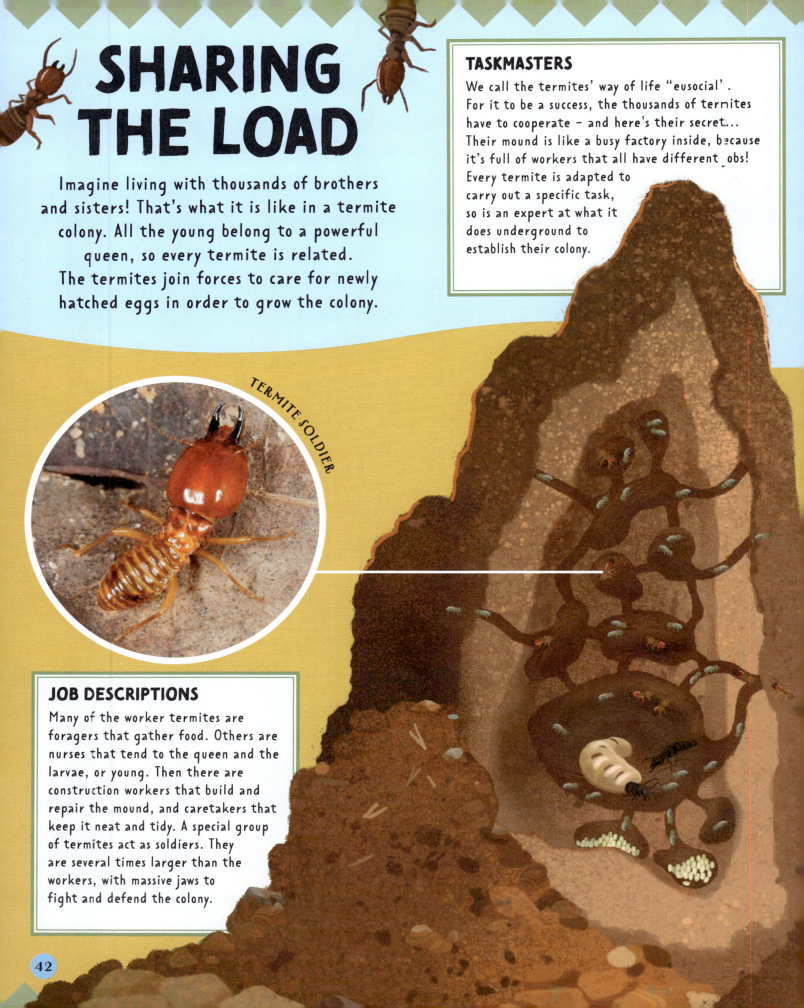

The queen lays eggs non-stop.

Workers carry the eggs to nursery chambers.

Some of these workers will tend the queen.

Eggs hatch into workers and soldiers.

SHARING THE LOAD

FIT FOR A QUEEN

Worker and soldier termites may be female or male, yet do not breed. All serve the queen termite, whose royal chamber is at the heart of the mound. She is a vast egg-laying "machine" that produces 30,000 eggs a day, adding up to millions of eggs over her long life. Her colossal body is so swollen, she can barely move. She is kept alive by her loyal workers.

TERMITE QUEEN

TERMITE WORKERS

In some cases, a queen termite may live for 50 years!

DAMARALAND MOLE RAT

Mole rats are the only vertebrates (animals with a backbone) whose lifestyle is similar to termites. There are two species, both of which are brilliant burrowers that spend most of the time underground. Damaraland mole rats form colonies with up to 25 members, and as with termites, each colony is controlled by a powerful queen. She is the only mole rat to produce young.

43

RIVAL CHEETAH

CHEETAHS

BANDS OF BROTHERS
Cheetah cubs become independent around 18 months old. Each sister starts a new life alone, whereas brothers stick together. There are two or three brothers in these "boy bands", or in some rare cases, up to five. Why hang out? The answer is that male cheetahs compete fiercely for territory, and in a group, the brothers are stronger, so can defend their area.

FIGHTING BACK

As soldiers know, if you find yourself under attack, it's good to have backup. The more of you there are, the better. It also pays to have a secret weapon to surprise and overwhelm your enemy.

GIANT HONEYBEES

ASIAN HORNET

GIVE ME A WAVE
Giant honeybees nest in tall trees out in the open where everyone can see them. Surely that's asking for trouble – won't other animals prey on their young or steal their delicious honey? But these bees have a trick to play on honey thieves and predators such as hornets. They lift their bodies, one after the other, to create waves that ripple across the swarm. The "shimmering" effect freaks out the thieves, which leave empty-handed.

DANGEROUS NEIGHBOURS

Why would you move in next to bad-tempered wasps? It seems a silly thing to do! Yet Montezuma oropendola birds love their company. They look for nests of warrior wasps and build their own nests alongside. The warrior wasps do them a favour by getting rid of troublesome botflies, whose larvae would otherwise feed on their chicks.

WARRIOR WASPS

FIGHTING BACK

Wood ants lack a sting – squirting acid is their main defence.

GREEN WOODPECKER

MONTEZUMA OROPENDOLA

SOUTHERN WOOD ANTS

SPRAY AWAY

Green woodpeckers have a taste for wood ants, but the ants fight back. Taking aim at their enemy's face, they all fire a jet of acid from the rear of their body. Pretty nasty! However, crows and jays actually ENCOURAGE the ants to spray them and even open their wings to get thoroughly soaked. These birds enjoy being showered in acid, because it kills the parasites in their feathers.

45

PROTECTIVE PARENTS

When you come face to face with wolves, what do you do? You could always just run for it... but for parent animals, that might not be the best way to save their babies. Savvy musk oxen stand their ground.

AFRICAN ELEPHANT

A young African elephant stays by its mother's side for more than three years. But despite the immense strength and loving protection of its supersized mum, the youngster is in constant danger. Lions can easily bring down an elephant calf. If the lions try to mount an attack, the elephant family bunch up in a circle, with their tusks facing outwards and the calf safely in the middle.

Wolves approach a musk ox calf.

The herd circles around it.

Beaten, the wolves retreat.

STANDING IN LINE

Musk oxen roam bogs and plains in the far north of the planet. In this frozen wilderness, called tundra, the bitter cold is not their main problem. It's wolves. A lone wolf is no bother – the musk oxen simply line up, so the wolf is met by a wall of sharp horns. The wolf cannot break this solid formation and slinks away. But a pack of wolves? That's a different matter...

PROTECTIVE PARENTS

MUSK OX CALF

HERD MENTALITY

When musk oxen encounter several wolves, they get into a circle. The young calves huddle in the centre, behind their mothers, because they are the weakest members of the herd – and the wolves' target. The adult musk oxen stand shoulder to shoulder, with their mighty horned heads facing outwards, so there is no easy way for the wolves to reach the vulnerable calves.

Both female and male musk oxen have horns. Their shaggy coats keep out the Arctic cold.

RESCUE ATTEMPT

Wolves are clever hunters and coordinate their hunts. Often they will split up and come at the musk oxen from different directions. If they can make the herd panic and start running, they will give chase, separate one of the slower calves, and quickly surround it. But all is not lost, because the rest of the herd may be able to come to its rescue and reform their defensive circle.

CALLING IN THE MOB

Uh-oh! If they see an intruder, some animals immediately kick up a tremendous fuss. By making an almighty racket, they can alert their friends, who rush over to help deal with the threat.

RALLYING ROUND

Many small birds raise the alarm when they see a predator. For example, if a black-capped chickadee notices an owl perched in the forest, it chatters at the top of its voice. Its calls rally other forest birds, which start calling too, and they band together to dart and dive at the owl. Eventually, the harrassed owl is fed up and flies off.

ALARM CALLS

We call this noisy behaviour "mobbing". The commotion is much like a burglar alarm going off – the predator has its cover blown. Now that everyone knows where it is, the predator is better off leaving. There's no point in staying, as its chances of surprising prey are zero. Some seabirds, such as gulls and terns, will also poo on unwelcome intruders so they really get the message!

GOLDEN-CROWNED KINGLET

BLACK-CAPPED CHICKADEE

BLUE JAY

EASTERN SCREECH OWL

CAPUCHIN MONKEY

CALLING IN THE MOB

SQUIRREL MONKEY

MONKEYING AROUND

In South American forests, common squirrel monkeys team up with capuchin monkeys. The different monkeys eat similar things – mainly insects, fruit, and other plant food – but there's plenty of grub to go round. And there are advantages to being in a big group. For one, there are more monkeys watching out for predators, especially snakes and harpy eagles.

I HEAR YOU

Amazingly, squirrel and capuchin monkeys understand each other's calls. If either species gives the danger signal, all the monkeys in the group know how to respond. They dive for cover pronto, or leap away through the treetops. As the capuchin monkeys are the biggest and boldest of the two, they may also pester a predator to drive it away. Naturally, this is a huge help to the smaller squirrel monkeys!

Squirrel monkeys can even ignore the calls of their own, in favour of the capuchin's.

CAPE GROUND SQUIRREL

These squirrels are found in dry areas of southern Africa, where their worst nightmare is the Cape cobra, a type of venomous snake. But, as the squirrels share a burrow, if one of them meets a cobra, it is able to whistle to the others for assistance. When they arrive on the scene and gang up on the cobra, it does not know which way to turn, so its strikes keep missing.

49

BLOOD MEALS

Horseflies drink blood – and not just from horses. They will bite many mammals for a blood meal, even humans! Blood is rich in protein and other nutrients, which is what the female flies need to produce their eggs. And the males? They're vegetarian! They can't bite, and would much rather sip sweet nectar from flowers, and plant juices known as sap.

HORSEFLIES

FEEDING PARASITES

The world is full of parasites that feed off the bodies of other animals – sometimes while they are still alive. To us, this may seem appalling behaviour, but it is a very successful way to live.

TARANTULA HAWK WASP

LIVING LUNCH

The female tarantula hawk wasp has the second most painful sting of any insect (only the bullet ant's sting hurts more). She uses it on a tarantula – but doesn't actually kill the great hairy spider. Instead, she paralyses it. Then she hauls the helpless beast to her burrow and lays a single egg on its body. This egg hatches into a larva, which eats the spider alive.

FEEDING PARASITES

BOTTOMS UP

Pearlfish have an odd relationship with sea cucumbers, which are seabed creatures that look nothing like real cucumbers. Each little pearlfish just swims up a sea cucumber's bottom! It shelters INSIDE the sausage-like body of its host, doing no harm. However, some kinds of pearlfish are altogether nastier. They're parasites that feast on their host's internal organs.

PEARLFISH IN LEOPARD SEA CUCUMBER

Pearlfish leave their host in order to find food... then swim right back up its bottom.

STICK AND SUCK

The candiru fish looks fairly harmless, but has a dark side. Found in South America, it lies in wait near the riverbed until it sniffs chemicals in the water that tell it a red-bellied piranha is passing. Quickly, it latches onto the gills of the piranha, using spines behind its head to stick into the flesh of the larger fish. Safely attached, the candiru sucks the blood of its host as it is carried along.

CANDIRU FISH

51

SNATCH OF THE DAY

A few crafty parasites steal food from other animals. But they don't hurt their victims directly. Like most parasites, the food thieves want their victims to survive – so they can continue stealing from them in the future!

LIFE OF CRIME

An Arctic skua circles over the ocean. Nearby, there is a colony of Atlantic puffins nesting on top of some cliffs. The skua is waiting for the parent puffins to return to the colony from their fishing trips. It doesn't have to wait long. Soon, the skua spies a puffin with its beak full of silvery sand eels, flying towards the cliffs to feed its chick. The chase is on!

ESCAPE MOVES

The skua has a long tail and wings that make it particularly fast and highly acrobatic in the air. Within moments, it has caught up with the alarmed puffin. In desperation, the puffin twists and turns to try and shake off its pursuer. But in doing so, it loses speed. The skua is far more powerful in flight, so the puffin's efforts are in vain.

DROP CATCH

Finally, the puffin opens its colourful beak and drops its fish, which the skua swoops to snatch. It's safer for the puffin to give up its hard-earned catch. On other occasions, the skua flies low over the waves as terns fish underwater. When these seabirds come to the surface, the skua pinches what they have caught. You may think the skua's behaviour is cruel, but like the puffins and terns, it too has chicks to feed.

SPOTTED HYENA

Hyenas are skilled hunters, but if they see an opportunity to steal their supper, they will. They particularly like to take meat from lions. Provided they outnumber the cats, they can get away with it. However, it's not as simple as that. The lions also steal meat from the hyenas. So, the lions and hyenas are both as "bad" as each other!

SNATCH OF THE DAY

These food thieves are called kleptoparasites, from a Greek word "klepto", meaning "steal".

ATLANTIC PUFFIN

ARCTIC SKUA

DISCO SNAIL

There are worms that can make snails act like zombies. Their extraordinary life begins in the snail's gut. From here, the young worms, or larvae, move into the snail's eyes. Then they use chemicals to force the snail to behave very oddly. Its eyestalks light up and pulse, like disco lights! The display attracts a bird, which thinks it has found a pair of wriggly caterpillars...

TREMATODE WORM LARVAE

AMBER SNAIL

ZOMBIE HOSTS

The sneakiest parasites use mind control. For their plan to work, they must invade the bodies of other animals. When they get inside, they turn their hosts into zombies that do whatever they want!

A snail eats thrush poo with worm eggs in it.

Worms breed in the thrush and release eggs.

Worm larvae make the snail's eyes flash.

Another thrush eats the snail.

COMPLETING THE CYCLE

The "caterpillars" certainly LOOK tasty, so the bird pulls the eyestalks off the zombie snail and eats them! This puts the worm larvae inside the bird, where they develop into adult worms. These breed and produce eggs. When the bird does a poo, the eggs are in it. The poo – with the eggs – is then eaten by a snail. The meal travels to the snail's gut, the eggs hatch, and so the worm life cycle begins again.

ZOMBIE HOSTS

HATCHING A PLAN

Horsehair worms turn crickets into zombies. The first part of their gruesome plan is to lay their eggs in water. The worm larvae that hatch are soon eaten by the larvae of mosquitoes, which also live in water. These grow into adult mosquitoes that fly around with the worm larvae still inside. The buzzy mosquitoes are tempting meals for crickets, and that suits the worm larvae...

HORSEHAIR WORM

DEATH LEAP

When a cricket eats a mosquito full of worm larvae, the larvae escape into its body and launch the next stage of their operation. They greedily feed on the insides of the cricket and take over its brain, probably with chemicals. Finally, they steer the zombie cricket towards some water, where it leaps in and drowns! The adult worms burst out of its body and breed, their plan complete.

COCKROACH WASP

The female emerald cockroach wasp is beautiful but deadly. She hunts for a cockroach and stings it in the brain. Her venom takes control of its mind. Then she buries her powerless victim and lays an egg. The wasp grub hatches and starts eating the zombie cockroach. As it remains alive, its flesh is nice and fresh!

FOSTER PARENTS

Every spring, the female brown-headed cowbird goes on a mission. She's looking for suitable foster parents for her young. Yellow warblers are ideal, so whenever she finds one of their nests, she quickly lays an egg and leaves. When the chick hatches, the parent yellow warblers are usually none the wiser. They rear the greedy cowbird chick as if it were one of their own, and even give it the most food – it grows bigger than they are!

BROOD PARASITES

In most birds, the eggs and young are looked after by mum or dad, or both parents together. But there are some, called brood parasites, where NEITHER parent does any actual parenting! They have a sly scheme to fool other species of birds into doing it for them.

BROWN-HEADED COWBIRD

YELLOW WARBLER

There's a cowbird egg in this yellow warbler nest...

...so the warblers put a new nest on top.

A NEW START

Ah, but what if the yellow warblers do spot what has happened? Well, as you can imagine, they are not happy. The thing is, a cowbird egg is too large for them to simply heave out of their nest. However, if they build another nest on top of the old one, it covers the unwanted egg, which then never hatches. A cunning way to defeat the cowbird's plan! The female yellow warbler then lays some new eggs.

BROOD PARASITES

ROUGH AND TUMBLE

Some of the most famous brood parasites are cuckoos. One of them, Horsfield's bronze cuckoo, lives in Australia and uses pretty little birds called fairywrens as foster parents. The chicks of Horsfield's bronze cuckoos are big bullies. Each grows up in a different fairywren nest, and wastes no time in chucking out all of the weaker fairywren chicks to get the nest to itself!

Fairywrens sing to their babies inside their eggs.

HORSFIELD'S BRONZE CUCKOO

Baby birds, just like human babies, can hear things before they are born.

SUPERB FAIRYWREN

PASSWORD PLEASE!

Parent fairywrens have found a way to defeat the cuckoos trying to invade their nest. The fairywren mum has a unique call that she sings to teach her babies while they are still developing in the eggs. Later, when the chicks hatch, they give this same call to ask for food. Because a cuckoo chick doesn't know this magic "password", the parents can tell something is wrong. They won't feed the unwelcome guest, and abandon it to start a new nest elsewhere.

CUCKOO PAPER WASP

Making a nest is way too much trouble for the female cuckoo paper wasp. She has other ideas – and barges her way into the nest of some European paper wasps. After a fight, she takes over the nest and starts to lay her own eggs. They hatch into grubs that deceive the nest's worker wasps into looking after them.

HELPFUL HOUNDS

Scientists think humans domesticated wolves between 27,000 and 40,000 years ago. From those early domestic dogs, we went on to breed several hundred different varieties of dog. Many breeds have characteristics that may help us in a particular way. Some, such as the Doberman, are bred for their protective nature. A well-cared-for Doberman will fiercely defend its human friends.

GUARD ANIMALS

We humans form incredible alliances with animals where both of us benefit. One of our first partnerships was with wolves, which we slowly domesticated to become dogs. Since then, we have offered a home to many other creatures that help us in return, often as guards.

DOBERMAN

LLAMA GUARDS

Llamas look like strange, long-legged sheep, but actually are cousins of camels. With a keen sense of hearing and smell, and excellent eyesight, these mammals don't miss much. The instant they notice an enemy (an eagle or a coyote, for example), they will rush over, spit in its direction, and make a dreadful sort of screech. They're so good at protecting sheep and goats that many farmers in South America employ llamas as guards.

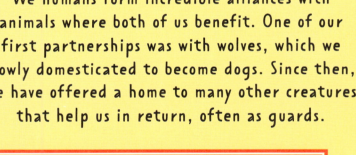

GUARDIAN LLAMA

GUARD ANIMALS

RED-LEGGED SERIEMA

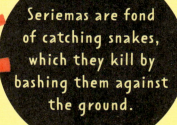

Seriemas are fond of catching snakes, which they kill by bashing them against the ground.

WHO GOES THERE?
Red-legged seriemas stalk the grasslands of Brazil and Argentina, where they hunt a wide range of small prey. They're wary birds, and if they sense danger, they shriek extremely loudly. This means they are handy as "guard dogs"! Chicken farmers in South America often look after a couple of seriemas, which return the favour by warning them about hawks that try to take their poultry.

ANGRY BIRDS
In the wild, geese protect their eggs and young by honking and hissing at their enemy, while beating their powerful wings. An angry goose means business! Though the display is mostly just for show, it deters all but the most persistent predators. The Romans were some of the first people to keep guard geese to raise the alarm, more than 2,000 years ago.

EGYPTIAN GOOSE

59

HONEY HUNTING

Ever dreamed of being able to talk to animals? It seems impossible. Yet in East Africa, it's a reality! People here team up with a clever species of bird, the greater honeyguide, and these unexpected allies really CAN communicate.

WILD HONEYBEE NEST

SHOW ME THE WAY

Wild honeybee nests take a bit of finding, because they are high up in trees, usually inside a branch or the trunk. But if the greater honeyguide finds one, it doesn't keep the discovery to itself. It first calls to attract the attention of people nearby, and then, by repeatedly flying a short way and calling again, it guides them to the nest. The honeyguide is like a feathery satnav!

SMOKE AND POKE

The human honey hunters climb the tree and, when the bees swarm out to defend their home blow smoke over the nest to calm them. Now the humans can reach into the nest to extract some of the honey. This is not what the honeyguide is after, though. It enjoys a tasty meal of young bees, or larvae, and eats the wax from which the honeycomb in the nest is made. Both partners in this deal are satisfied.

HONEY HUNTING

TEAM CHATS
The alliance between humans and the greater honeyguide is found only in parts of Kenya, Tanzania, and Mozambique. Studies show that in these areas, the honeyguide uses squeaky calls to "talk" to local people. When they whistle to the bird, it also understands them. This is a rare example of a wild creature and humans chatting and working as a team.

The greater honeyguide is a brood parasite, which means it gets other birds to raise its young.

HONEYGUIDE

COMMON EIDER
Female eider ducks line their nests with fluffy under-feathers called down, including some they pluck from their own breast. Wonderfully soft and warm, the eider down keeps the eggs cosy. For centuries, people in Iceland and Norway have taken this down to fill jackets, pillows, and bed covers. If they collect it after the nesting season, the ducks don't come to any harm.

FORAGING TOGETHER

Since ancient times, humans and animals have joined forces to hunt and fish. Many of these astonishing alliances have died out and can no longer be seen, but a few survive to this day.

GOLDEN EAGLE

Hunters wear a tough leather glove to avoid being hurt by their eagle's claws.

WINGING IT

Cave paintings more than 4,000 years old show people using trained birds of prey to hunt. A traditional version of this type of hunting continues in Mongolia, where a few Kazakh families still hunt with golden eagles, the way they always have. Each hunter trains their eagle to soar away, catch a hare or fox, and bring it back to their fist. Afterwards, the eagle gets some meat and the hunter usually keeps the animal's fur.

TRUST ME

Kazakh hunters develop a close bond with their eagle. Gradually, the bird learns to trust its human trainer, who in turn must remember it is not a pet, but a working partner. The relationship is similar to that of a farmer and their sheepdog. There are concerns that taking young eagles from the wild might threaten the eagle population, but a hunter only keeps their eagle a few years, then returns it to the wild so it can breed.

FORAGING TOGETHER

IRRAWADDY DOLPHIN

MAKING A SPLASH

Dolphins like to follow boats and leap about in the waves they create, which may partly be for fun. But Irrawaddy dolphins approach boats for a different reason. Found in rivers in Southeast Asia, they have learned that it pays to go fishing with local villagers. The human fishers simply tap the sides of their boat to ask these unusual little dolphins for help!

NET FLICKS

Alerted by the tapping, the dolphins swim in circles to drive fish towards the fishers' boat. A net is hurled into the water, which begins filling with fish. The dolphins win too, as they're able to snatch fish confused by the movement of the net. Sadly, Irrawaddy dolphins are endangered. Unless their river habitat is better protected, they might become extinct and this human-dolphin partnership will come to an end.

SMOOTH-COATED OTTER

People in Bangladesh, South Asia, breed these otters and train them to chase fish into a net. The human fishers take the trained otters with them in their fishing boat, then put their net in the river and release the otters. Superb swimmers, the otters spread out to herd fish into the net, in return for fishy treats later.

63

WHAT'S THE BUZZ?
Many bees are FANTASTIC at carrying pollen between different flowers (we call this pollination). The pollen sticks well to their hairy bodies. Bumblebees actually hold onto flowers and buzz their wings so hard to extract the pollen, that they get showered in the stuff! The bees then pollinate the flowers of crops such as tomatoes and potatoes, being rewarded with pollen and nectar from the plants.

BUFF-TAILED BUMBLEBEE

FREAKY BEAKS
Hummingbirds never stay still for long. They zoom about the place, using their long beak and tongue to reach into flowers and sip the nectar waiting for them. Sword-billed hummingbirds own a beak up to 12 cm (4.7 in) in length, which is actually longer than their body! They push it deep inside tube-like flowers, such as the angel's trumpet, to sip the nectar at the bottom. By flitting between flowers, the hummingbirds pollinate them.

SWORD-BILLED HUMMINGBIRD

ANIMALS & PLANTS

Animals and plants have long worked as a team. Most plants reproduce using flowers, which attract animals that then carry a substance called pollen to more flowers. As a thank you, the plants feed their animal helpers with sugary liquid nectar, and sometimes with a bit of the pollen, too.

ANIMALS & PLANTS

The flowers of balsa trees close during the day and open at night, when bats are active.

GREATER SPEAR-NOSED BAT

MIDNIGHT FEAST

After dark in Australia, you can see mouse-like creatures scurrying around bushes and trees. These are honey possums, which have an exceptionally pointy nose for feeding from flowers. The tip of their tongue is shaped like a brush to sweep the nectar and pollen right into their mouth. While the possums feed, they become covered in sticky pollen. So, as they move from flower to flower, they pollinate the blooms.

BALSA BATS

Lots of bats are insect-eaters, but in tropical regions, there are also many that feast on nectar and pollen. One such bat is the greater spear-nosed bat. It's a very large bat and loves to feed from the flowers of balsa trees, pollinating them as it does so. Groups of flying bats call to each other – scientists think they may be swapping information about where the nearest balsa trees are.

HONEY POSSUM

PLANT TOXINS

Plants are forever being munched by vegetarian animals. So, to avoid turning into someone's lunch, many plants are poisonous. But the poisons don't affect some creatures, which can absorb them and become toxic, too!

MONARCH BUTTERFLY LARVA

MONARCH BUTTERFLY

GET AWAY FROM ME!

Milkweed is stuffed with poison, yet the caterpillars of monarch butterflies are immune to it (they are naturally protected). They can chomp the plant to their heart's content, and soon become toxic themselves. The poisons remain when they turn into butterflies, which are equally lethal. In this relationship, the milkweed loses. Its leaves are munched, its poison is "stolen", and it receives nothing in return.

Monarch butterflies feed on the nectar of milkweed, but don't pollinate the flowers.

PLANT TOXINS

LEARNING A LESSON

If a bird catches a monarch butterfly, it instantly spits out the unpleasant meal. It remembers the butterfly's colourful appearance so it doesn't make the same mistake in the future. Many other toxic animals, from bugs to frogs, also have bold colours and patterns to alert predators that they are dangerous. We call this "warning coloration".

CASSIN'S KINGBIRD

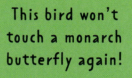

This bird won't touch a monarch butterfly again!

MILKWEED BUGS

MILKWEED TUSSOCK MOTH

MILKWEED ON THE MENU

Several other insects can feed on milkweed and absorb its toxins. They all have warning coloration. Milkweed bugs, for example, are bright-red and black, and the caterpillars of milkweed tussock moths are stripy with white tufts of hair sticking out in every direction. Scientists think these insects developed their resistance to the milkweed toxins over a long period of time.

PAINTED GRASSHOPPER

As a rule, grasshoppers are green or brown. Their camouflage colours hide them among grasses and other plants. But the painted grasshopper is the complete opposite! Its flashy colours make it stand out – and are a warning that it has gobbled down plant toxins and stored them in its body.

SEED DISPERSAL

How do plants, which are rooted to the spot, spread their seeds? The answer is, they have to get creative! Many enlist animals to transport the seeds – and offer lavish amounts of food as payment.

HIDE AND SEEK

In autumn, Steller's jays gather thousands of pine tree seeds, but don't eat them straight away. These smart birds carry the seeds elsewhere in their throat, up to 20 at a time, to bury in the soil. Months later, if they're hungry, they return to their seed stores for a much-needed meal. But though the jays memorize where their treasure is hidden, they can't remember every hiding place...

TREE PLANTING

The seeds that the jays forget about will germinate, or sprout, into pine tree seedlings. In this way, the jays help the pine trees to spread. And, because the jays may fly several kilometres before burying their seeds, they help the forest to spread, too. The jays are rewarded with seedy snacks, the pine trees get to reproduce, and the forest expands. A winning partnership!

STELLER'S JAY

SEED DISPERSAL

RED-RUMPED AGOUTI

BRAZIL NUTS

CRACKING JOB
Some nuts are harder to crack than others, and the outer case of a Brazil nut is so hard that agoutis are among the few animals able to chew through it to reach the seeds inside. When food is plentiful, these rodents will bury the seeds to eat later, but if they forget where their treats are hidden, the seeds grow into new Brazil nut trees. In this two-way relationship, the agoutis and trees both come out tops.

ORANGUTAN
Orangutans scatter seeds as they travel through the rainforest. And the way they do it is... by going to the toilet. Whenever they eat fruit, they digest the sweet flesh, but the seeds are too tough and pass through their stomach and gut unharmed. So, their poo delivers seeds to the forest floor, ready to grow.

As in all rodents, the front teeth of agoutis never stop growing, which keeps them sharp.

WILD HARVEST
Humans eat Brazil nuts, too. But Brazil nut trees are difficult to grow on farms, so we mostly harvest the nuts from wild trees in forests. The nuts are a valuable natural product that earn millions of dollars a year for several South American countries. This makes the job of the agoutis important for local people, as well as the forest ecosystem.

69

SETTLING IN

Like the best hotels and restaurants, certain plants want their guests to feel comfortable. Except their guests are animals, not humans! Their customers have some bizarre ways of paying the bill, too...

The pitcher plant nectar contains a substance that makes its guests need the toilet.

MOUNTAIN TREE SHREW

PLEASE BE SEATED

Most pitcher plants are meat-eaters. They lure insects with their sweet scent and nectar, then drown their visitors in digestive juices and eat them. But Low's pitcher plant treats its guests much better. It makes a luxurious seat for a mouse-like animal called the mountain tree shrew, whose bottom fits snugly over the top of the "bowl" formed by its unusual leaves.

The tree shrew climbs onto the pitcher plant to feed...

...it poos, and leaves.

SHREW ON THE LOO

The tree shrew sits on the pitcher plant, greedily licks the nectar, and as it does so, relieves itself. The poo falls into the plant's "bowl", the shape of which might remind you of a toilet. And that's because... this weird plant IS a toilet! It drains the poo, which is full of nutrients such as nitrogen that the soil here lacks. So, the pitcher plant and tree shrew both end up well-fed!

LOW'S PITCHER PLANT

SETTLING IN

GILA WOODPECKER

Woodpeckers are famous for pecking holes in trees. Yet the Gila woodpecker lives in the deserts of Mexico and Southwest USA, where there are hardly any trees to be seen. Instead it nests in saguaro cacti, which grow as tall as two-storey houses and can be up to 200 years old. The woodpecker is somehow able to dodge the spines to make a homely nesting hole.

SAGUARO CACTUS

Other animals, such as elf owls, live in any abandoned nest holes.

PAYING RENT

The Gila woodpecker's nest hole is up to 50 cm (19.5 in) deep, so causes quite a lot of harm to the cactus. But the bird repays the cactus twice over. First, it eats bugs that infest and damage the cactus. And second, it eats the cactus fruit, carrying the seeds away inside its gut to poo out elsewhere in the desert. The seeds may sprout into new cacti one day, helping the plant to spread.

GILA WOODPECKER

RED-EYED TREE FROG

Female red-eyed tree frogs lay their eggs on tree leaves to keep them safe. They choose leaves hanging over ponds, so when the eggs hatch, the tadpoles can drop off and fall into the water below. The leaves also serve as umbrellas during tropical downpours! The trees don't benefit from any of this, but helping the frogs doesn't cost them anything either.

71

CLAWSOME COMPANIONS

The deep ocean is the haunt of ghostly white creatures called yeti crabs. See that long hair on their body and claws? It's covered in delicious bacteria that the crabs nibble as food. The crabs like to wave their claws around. Perhaps they do this dance to churn up the water. That might wash fresh supplies of oxygen and other nutrients over the bacteria, helping them grow.

YETI CRAB

BACTERIA BEST FRIENDS

Too small to see with the naked eye, bacteria are tiny living things made of a single cell. They are found on and in the bodies of animals in vast numbers, and in return for their free accommodation, they can give their hosts "superpowers".

SHINING BRIGHT

How do you catch your dinner in the deep ocean where it's totally dark? The female anglerfish has come up with a brilliant solution. She has live-in bacteria that create their own light. This superpower is called bioluminescence (you say it "bye-oh-loo-mi-ness-ens"). The bacteria live at the tip of a spine on her forehead and light up to attract prey towards her mouth.

ANGLERFISH

72

BACTERIA BEST FRIENDS

VANISHING ACT

The Hawaiian bobtail squid is around the size of an adult human's thumb, which is tiny for a squid. To help it hide, it has an organ filled with glowing bacteria. Their glow matches the glimmer of light from the Moon and stars above, so the squid's shadow disappears, making it seem "invisible". Now the little squid can sneak up on prey, and escape its enemies!

HAWAIIAN BOBTAIL SQUID

Humans also house friendly bacteria. There are trillions in your gut that help to digest food.

PROBOSCIS MONKEY

THE MUNCH BUNCH

Leaves can be difficult to digest, as they're packed with tough plant material called fibre, as well as toxins. Despite this, leaves are the proboscis monkey's favourite food. It has a very large, bulging stomach similar to that of a cow, with four main chambers, all home to friendly bacteria. These leaf-munching allies break down the plant fibre for the monkey and make the toxins safe.

73

THE CORAL & THE ALGAE

To see one of the greatest partnerships in nature, we need to dive to the ocean floor. Here, there are beautiful reefs made of colourful coral, which rely on live-in algae to survive.

BLEACHED CORAL

CORAL COMMUNITY

Coral can look like trees, ferns, mushrooms, brains, or even the antlers of deer. These amazing structures are built from mind-blowing numbers of tiny animals called coral polyps. Each of the polyps sits in a stony skeleton a bit like an eggcup. The polyps link up with their neighbours to make a single structure, or colony. Lots of coral colonies may join up to create a reef.

ZOOXANTHELLAE

SOLAR ENERGY

Coral polyps are see-through, which means sunlight can reach inside their bodies, where algae are living. The algae use the energy in the sunlight to make food (this is a process called photosynthesis, and plants do it, too). The algae share their food with the coral they live with. Scientists believe that coral and algae have lived together like this for as long as 210 million years.

THE CORAL & THE ALGAE

CORAL BLEACHING

Sadly, the relationship between the coral and the algae may break down. One of the main causes is climate change, which makes seawater warmer and more acidic. When this happens, coral becomes stressed and the polyps force their algae out. As their gorgeous colours came from the algae, they now appear white and "bleached". And, with their main source of food gone, they soon die.

GIANT CLAM

This mammoth sea creature is a mollusc related to oysters and mussels. Like them, it has a pair of shells joined at a hinge. Unlike them, it's the biggest mollusc on Earth! But WHY does it grow so large? The giant clam's secret is a community of helpful algae. These allies live in the clam's bright blue insides, make their own food, and share it with the clam.

The algae that live in coral are called zooxanthellae (you say it "zoo-zanth-ell-ee").

75

CROP FARMING

People probably began farming around 12,000 years ago. But leafcutter ants have been doing it MUCH longer than that. For millions of years, they have farmed fungus, which they harvest as food.

The ants carry leaf cuttings in their powerful jaws.

FUNGUS GARDENS

Leafcutter ants live in the forests of Central and South America, where they look after fungus gardens to feed themselves and their larvae, or young. The gardens are underground in their enormous nest. Trails of worker ants march into the forest to cut up fresh green leaves that they carry back to make a kind of fertilizer for their beloved fungus.

A leafcutter ant can carry a leaf weighing 20 times its own body weight.

TENDER CARE

In the nest, there may be several million ants tending to their curious crop. They stroke the fungus clean, carry away bits of rubbish that get in its way, and dig up other kinds of fungus that try to grow there, like gardeners doing the weeding. The ants even sprinkle the fungus gardens with a special liquid from their bottom! It keeps the area free from harmful mould and pests.

CROP FARMING

TOP OF THE CROPS

The leafcutter ants bring their humongous fungus up to 50,000 leaves a day! In return, it produces lots of tiny stalks, like a crop of strange fruit. The ants eat these "fruit" greedily, as they are rich in fat and carbohydrate, and also feed them to their larvae. The fungus likes it so much in the ant nest, it now lives nowhere else – and that suits the ants just fine, because without the helpful and rather tasty fungus, their colony would soon die out.

The ants harvest their nutritious crop.

FUNGUS

The ants use the cuttings to make fertilizer.

DUSKY DAMSELFISH

Ants aren't the only farmers. Above all else, dusky damselfish love to eat red algae. To make sure they never run out, they grow patches of it on the coral reef. All day they patrol up and down, chasing away other fish that dare to nibble the algae. Using their mouth as a spade, they weed out other types of algae to give their crop more growing room. For the farmer fish and the algae, it's a win-win situation.

77

INDEX

A

African elephants 46
African wild dogs 38-39
agoutis 69
algae 32, 33 74-75, 77
   red 77
   zooxanthellae 74, 75
amber snails 54
anemones 20
animal babysitters 38, 39, 41
animal crèches/nurseries 36-37
ants 7, 14, 15, 31, 45, 50, 76, 77
aphids 14, 15
apolemia uvaria 23
Arctic foxes 9
Asian hornets 44

B

baboons 40
bacteria 72-73
badgers 31
bait ball 12
banded mongooses 41
bats 9, 65
bees 7, 28, 30, 44, 60, 64
bioluminescence 72
birds
   Arctic skuas 52, 53
   Atlantic puffins 52, 53
   black-capped chickadees 48
   blue jays 48
   brown-headed cowbirds 56
   burrowing owls 19
   Cape gannets 13
   Cassin's kingbirds 67
   crows 45
   eastern screech owls 48
   Egyptian geese 59
   eider ducks 61
   elf owls 71
   emperor penguins 36
   European robins 8
   fairywrens 57
   Gila woodpeckers 71
   golden-crowned kinglets 48
   golden eagles 62
   greater flamingos 37
   greater honeyguides 60-61
   green woodpeckers 45
   Harris's hawks 11
   Horsfield's bronze cuckoos 57
   jays 45
   kori bustards 28
   long-tailed tits 41
   Montezuma oropendolas 45
   of prey 11, 62
   pygmy falcons 16
   red-billed oxpeckers 35
   red-legged seriemas 59
   royal terns 36
   sociable weavers 16
   southern carmine bee-eaters 28
   Steller's jays 68
   sword-billed hummingbirds 64
   terns 8, 52
   yellow warblers 56
biting flies 9
black-and-white ruffed lemurs 37
black rhinos 35
botflies 45
breeding 22
bromeliads 7
burrows 18-19
burying beetles 27
butterflies
   Adonis blue 15
   monarch butterfly 66, 67
   purple hairstreak 15

C

caimans 30
Cape cobras 49
Cape fur seals 13
Cape ground squirrels 49
capuchin monkeys 49
caterpillars 15, 66, 67
cheetahs 44
climate change 75
colonies 6, 16-17, 22, 42, 43
common marmosets 39
corals 21, 32, 33, 74-75, 77
   bleaching 74, 75
   colony 74
   polyps 74, 75
   reefs 32, 33, 74, 77
crabs 24, 72
crickets 19, 55
crop farming 76-77

D

Damaraland mole rats 43
dholes 11
dogs 58
dolphins 12, 63
   common 12
   Irrawaddy 63
dragonflies 28

E

eastern diamondback
   rattlesnakes 19

F

fish
   angelfish 33
   anglerfish 72
   barbel fish 35
   bluebottle fish 23
   blue rockfish 7
   candiru fish 51
   clownfish 20
   damselfish 33
   dusky damselfish 77
   goliath groupers 25
   mackerels 8
   manta rays 32
   moon wrasses 32, 33
   pearlfish 51
   red-bellied piranhas 51
   remoras 34
   sand eels 52
   sardines 12, 13
   sharks 13, 34
   surgeonfish 33
   yellowfin tunas 8
   yellow tangs 32, 33
fishing 63
Florida mice 19
frogs 7, 19, 71
fungus gardens 76, 77

G

giant anteaters 17
giant armadillos 19
giant clams 75
glass sponges 21
glass sponge shrimps 21
gopher tortoises 18, 19
gopher tortoise rove beetles 19
ground squirrels 17

H

harlequin beetles 26, 27
Hawaiian bobtail squids 73
hippopotamuses 35
honeydew 14, 15
honey possums 65
horseflies 50
horsehair worms 55
hyenas 35, 41, 53

L

ladybirds 14
lions 35, 38, 46, 53
llamas 58

M

mega-brood 40
milkweed 66, 67
milkweed bugs 67
milkweed tussock moths 67
mites, red 27
mobbing 48, 49
mole skinks 19
mosquitoes 28, 55
mountain tree shrews 70
musk oxen 46-47

78

O

ocelots 19
orangutans 69
orcas 10
ostriches 40

P

painted grasshoppers 67
paper nautilus octopuses 25
parasites 7, 25, 27, 33, 34, 35, 50-51, 52- 53, 54-55
    brood parasites 56-57, 60, 61
    kleptoparasites 7, 53
phoresy 26, 27
photosynthesis 74
plants 64, 65, 66, 67, 70, 71, 73
polar bears 9
pollination 64, 65
Portuguese man-of-wars 22, 23
proboscis monkeys 73
pseudoscorpions 26, 27
pygmy seahorses 21

S

saguaro cacti 71
Sardine Run 12
sea cucumbers 51
seals 10
sea urchins 24
seed dispersal 68-69, 71
    Brazil nuts 69
    pine trees 68
silica 21
siphonophores 22, 23
smooth-coated otters 63
spotted skunks 19
squirrel monkeys 49
symbiosis 6-7
    colonial 6, 7
    commensalism 6, 7
    eusocial 7, 42
    mutualism 6, 7
    parasitism 6, 7

T

tarantulas 50
tentacles 22, 23
termites 7, 17, 42-43
terrapins 28
ticks 35
tiger beetles 19
trematode worms 54
turtles 32, 33

V

venom 19, 22, 23, 24, 55
Venus's flower baskets 21

W

warning coloration 67
wasps 7, 14, 16, 28, 45, 50, 55, 57
Weddell seals 10
whales
    barnacles 29
    Bryde's whale 12, 13
    humpback whales 13, 29
white-tailed deer 9
wild boars 8
wolves 46-47, 58

Z

zooids 22

ABOUT THE AUTHOR

BEN HOARE is a science writer and editor, and the author of the hugely successful *An Anthology of Intriguing Animals*, as well as *The Wonders of Nature*, *Nature's Treasures*, *The Secret World of Plants*, *Weird and Wonderful Nature*, and *An Anthology of Exquisite Birds* for DK. He is passionate about nature and sharing his knowledge of the natural world.

ABOUT THE ILLUSTRATOR

ASIA ORLANDO is a digital artist, illustrator, and environmentalist. Asia creates artwork for books, magazines, products, and posters. Her work focuses on harmony between animals, humans, and the environment. She's also the founder of Our Planet Week, a social media event for illustrators aimed to address environmental issues.

ACKNOWLEDGEMENTS

The publisher would like to thank the following for their kind permission to reproduce their photographs:

(Key: a-above; b-below/bottom; c-centre; f-far; l-left; r-right; t-top)

6 123RF.com: Agm0608 (tr). **Alamy Stock Photo:** Paul Markillie (cl); Nature Picture Library / Ingo Arndt (bc). **7 Alamy Stock Photo:** Krystyna Szulecka Photography (tc); Nature Picture Library / David Hall (cr). **Dreamstime.com:** Hilmawan Nurhatmadi (bl). **8 Alamy Stock Photo:** Biosphoto / Sergio Hanquet (cla). **Shutterstock.com:** Bildagentur Zoonar GmbH (br). **9 Alamy Stock Photo:** Linda Freshwaters Arndt (br). **Dreamstime.com:** Agami Photo Agency (tr). **10 naturepl.com:** Bertie Gregory (c). **11 naturepl.com:** Jack Dykinga (c). **12-13 Alamy Stock Photo:** VWPics / David Salvatori (c). **13 Shutterstock.com:** Wildestanimal (crb). **14 Warren Photographic Limited:** (t). **15 Alamy Stock Photo:** Dom Greves (t). **16 Alamy Stock Photo:** Avalon.red / Martin Harvey (bc); Nature Picture Library / Alan Williams (tr). **17 Alamy Stock Photo:** Animal Stock (cra); Rosanne Tackaberry (bl). **18 Alamy Stock Photo:** Minden Pictures / Pete Oxford. **20 Alamy Stock Photo:** Hans Gert Broeder (c). **21 naturepl.com:** David Shale (tc, c). **23 Alamy Stock Photo:** Biosphoto / Sergio Hanquet (c); Nature Photographers Ltd / Paul R. Sterry. **24 Alamy Stock Photo:** Nature Picture Library / Constantinos Petrinos (tl). **Getty Images:** Moment / Antonio Luis Martinez Cano (bc). **25 Alamy Stock Photo:** Chris Gug (crb). **naturepl.com:** Magnus Lundgren (tl). **26-27 Alamy Stock Photo:** Stock Connection Blue / Loren McIntyre (t). **28 naturepl.com:** Richard Du Toit (c). **29 Alamy Stock Photo:** FishHook Photography (bc); WaterFrame_mus (r). **30 Alamy Stock Photo:** Arterra Picture Library / Clement Philippe (tr); Rolf Nussbaumer Photography / Stefan Huwiler / Rolfnp (cl). **31 Alamy Stock Photo:** Zoonar / Manfred Rogl (cl). **Shutterstock.com:** Russell Marshall (cr). **32-33 Alamy Stock Photo:** Blue Planet Archive BPD. **33 Alamy Stock Photo:** Blue Planet Archive (tl). **34 Alamy Stock Photo:** SeaTops (c). **Getty Images:** Universal Images Group / Education Images (cb). **35 Alamy Stock Photo:** Nature Picture Library / Pal Hermansen (c). **36 Alamy Stock Photo:** All Canada Photos / Wayne Lynch (bl); Dawna Moore (cra). **37 Alamy Stock Photo:** PA Images / Barry Batchelor (br). **Dreamstime.com:** Slowmotiongli (tl). **38-39 Alamy Stock Photo:** Martin Chapman. **39 Alamy Stock Photo:** Nature Picture Library / Karine Aigner (tl). **40 naturepl.com:** Klaus Nigge (b). **41 naturepl.com:** Anup Shah (c). **42 Shutterstock.com:** RealityImages (cl). **43 Alamy Stock Photo:** Minden Pictures / Mitsuhiko Imamori (c). **44 Dreamstime.com:** Beijada (crb); Stu Porter (tl). **45 Alamy Stock Photo:** www.pqpictures.co.uk (bl). **Getty Images:** The Image Bank / Gerard Soury (cr). **46-47 Alamy Stock Photo:** Minden Pictures / Jim Brandenburg. **47 Alamy Stock Photo:** All Canada Photos / Wayne Lynch (tl). **48 Alamy Stock Photo:** E.R. Degginger (b). **Science Photo Library:** Edward Kinsman (cra). **49 Alamy Stock Photo:** F1online digitale Bildagentur GmbH / David & Micha Sheldon (tr); imageBROKER.com GmbH & Co. KG / Sohns (tl). **50 Alamy Stock Photo:** Rick & Nora Bowers (bl); Ros Crosland (tl). **51 Alamy Stock Photo:** VWPics / Jorge García (bl). **Science Photo Library:** Georgette Douwma (tr). **52-53 naturepl.com:** Espen Bergersen. **54 Shutterstock.com:** Henri Koskinen (l). **55 Alamy Stock Photo:** Andrea Battisti (c); Ephotocorp / Ashok Captain (cl). **56 Alamy Stock Photo:** E.R. Degginger (c). **57 Keith Wilcox:** (c). **58 Alamy Stock Photo:** Sipa USA / Paul Tople / Akron Beacon Journal / MCT (br). **Dreamstime.com:** Archangel80889 (tr). **59 Alamy Stock Photo:** Duncan Usher (br). **Dreamstime.com:** Dalia Kvedaraite (cla). **60 Alamy Stock Photo:** Jeremy ODonnell (tr). **60-61 naturepl.com:** Roland Seitre. **62 Shutterstock.com:** MehmetO (b). **63 Alamy Stock Photo:** Patty Tse (t). **naturepl.com:** Roland Seitre (tl). **64 Getty Images / iStock:** Ajcespedes (tr). **naturepl.com:** Jim Clare (clb). **65 naturepl.com:** Jiri Lochman (br); Christian Ziegler (cl). **66 Alamy Stock Photo:** Dembinsky Photo Associates / Skip Moody (tr). **66-67 Getty Images:** Moment / Katrin Ray Shumakov. **68 Alamy Stock Photo:** William Leaman. **69 Alamy Stock Photo:** Nature Picture Library / Robin Chittenden (t). **Getty Images / iStock:** Edsongrandisoli (cl). **70 Science Photo Library:** Paul Williams (r). **71 Alamy Stock Photo:** Dave Watts (r). **Dreamstime.com:** Winnietam (tc). **72 Alamy Stock Photo:** Nature Picture Library / David Shale (br). **naturepl.com:** David Shale (tl). **73 Alamy Stock Photo:** Chris Hellier (bl). **Getty Images:** Moment Open / Steven Trainoff Ph.D. (tr). **74 Alamy Stock Photo:** imageBROKER.com GmbH & Co. KG / J.W.Alker (tr). **74-75 Alamy Stock Photo:** David Fleetham. **76-77 naturepl.com:** Martin Dohrn (b). **77 Dreamstime.com:** Aaron66zc (cra)

Cover images: *Front:* **Alamy Stock Photo:** Reinhard Dirscherl tr, Stu Porter bl; **Getty Images / iStock:** RichLindie br; **naturepl.com:** Doug Perrine tl; *Back:* **Alamy Stock Photo:** Blue Planet Archive CMA-X tr, E.R. Degginger bl; **Getty Images / iStock:** Eric Yeamans br; **Shutterstock.com:** Cheryl Thomas tl

All other images © Dorling Kindersley

Ben would like to thank

Every book is a partnership and this one could not have been created without the brilliant creative team at DK. A huge round of applause to my editor Abi Maxwell, ably assisted by James Mitchem, and to the entire design team – Charlotte Milner, Bettina Myklebust Stovne, Brandie Tully-Scott and Victoria Palastanga. I've said it before, but you're the best in the business!

Asia Orlando, your artwork is always a delight. Your illustrations are so witty and joyful! Thanks too to my amazing agent Gill McClay.

It is a huge privilege to write about the natural world for a living. So finally I would also like to thank the many wonderful animals, plants, fungi, and other living things featured in these pages.

DK would like to thank

Gabriel Midgley for design assistance; Laura Gilbert for proofreading; Claire Sipi for indexing; and Sakshi Saluja and Samrajkumar S for picture research.